THE
DRIVING TEST
STUDY AID

THE DRIVING TEST STUDY AID

by
ANDREW CROUCH A.D.I., M.I.A.M.
and
JOSEPH LEVINE A.D.I.

W. Foulsham & Company Limited
Yeovil Road, Slough, Berkshire, SL1 4JH

ISBN 0-572-01429-5

Printed in Great Britain at
St Edmundsbury Press, Bury St Edmunds

CONTENTS

Colour is represented
in diagrams and Highway
Code symbols as shown in
the boxes below

Red

Blue

Diagrams have been adapted from
The Highway Code with the permission
of the Controller of Her Majesty's
Stationery Office.

INTRODUCTION

Much unnecessary fear is attached to the driving test mainly because it is a unique experience. There is no other situation in life where your every action will be watched so closely by another person.

In this book we hope to eliminate this fear by showing you exactly what is required. It will not make you a driver — only practical experience can do that. It will, however, teach you how to drive and help you pass the test.

As with any examination, it is most important to prepare oneself and not just turn up on the day hoping for the best. Current statistics show that less than 50 per cent of candidates pass the test in any one year and, with nearly two million people taking the test, that is a staggering one million 'fails' each year. Although the specific reasons people fail the test are many, the overriding factor is that people are not ready. Driving is a skill and any skill can be mastered by applying oneself to it in the proper manner.

By the time you take the driving test, you should be able to understand everything in this book and be confident that you could handle all the situations mentioned.

1
PLANNING FOR A TEST

Q *How do I apply for a driving test?*
A Go to any post office and ask for a driving test application form. Take care when completing it to read each question carefully. There are explanatory notes to assist you.

Q *Can I take the test at a centre of my own choosing?*
A Yes. The back of the application form lists all the driving test centres and you can choose any one of these.

Q *Can I take the test if I am disabled?*
A Yes, but you must declare your disability on the application form, and to the examiner prior to the test.

Q *What are the age limits for taking the test in a motor-car?*

A You must be at least 17 but there is no upper age limit.

Q *Can I take the test in an automatic car?*

A Yes, but this means that on passing the test you can only drive an automatic car.

Q *Can I use my own car for the test?*

A Yes, provided everything is legal and in proper working order, and the seat-belts are clean.

Q *Do I need to understand the workings of the car?*

A This is not necessary but you should be familiar with the interior layout of the car, e.g. where the hazard warning lights and the horn are situated.

Q *What do I need to take with me on the day of the test?*

A Your driving licence, your test appointment card and, if you are taking the test in your own car, your insurance details.

Q *How long does the test last?*

A Usually tests take place every 45 minutes, but this includes some time for the examiner to complete the necessary paperwork. You will be expected to drive for approximately 30 minutes, then the examiner will ask you several questions.

Generally, speaking from start to finish, about 35 minutes will be spent in the vehicle.

Q *How early should I arrive at the test centre?*
A Allow enough time to find a suitable parking place and to prepare yourself. Rushing prior to the test will only hinder your performance.

Q *Are there toilets at every test centre?*
A No, but there will be some nearby.

Q *Are tests conducted at night or at weekends?*
A No. All tests are taken during office hours.

Q *Is there a quota of passes?*
A No. You will pass or fail on your own ability.

Q *Can I choose my examiner?*
A No. The tests are allocated on a random basis.

Q *Are there any female examiners?*
A Yes, there are a few.

Q *Does it help to know the test area?*
A It helps to have a general idea but it is not strictly necessary. Do not confine yourself just to the test area but prior to taking the test, ensure you have enough practice on all types of road.

Q *Do examiners always follow the same route?*
A No. There are lots of routes and these are varied from test to test.

Q *How should I dress?*
A You must feel comfortable. The examiner will not be influenced in any way by your style of dress.

Q *Can I drive in bare feet?*
A Yes, if you find it more comfortable, but it is not advisable.

Q *Can someone sit in the back of the car during the test?*
A Yes, with the examiner's permission. If you have difficulty with the language, it may help to have an interpreter. Some candidates like to have their own driving instructor in the car, but remember, he must take no part in the test. Note that on some tests, a supervising examiner may be present but he will have no influence on the result.

Q *What books should I read to help me pass the test?*
A When you receive your provisional driving licence, you will also receive a copy of the Highway Code and a leaflet entitled *Your Driving Test*. Both these booklets must be read thoroughly. There are numerous books to help your driving. One of these is published by the Department of the

Environment and is entitled *Driving*.
Another book you will find useful is *Your
Highway Code Test Made Easy* by Brenda
Ralph Lewis, published by W. Foulsham.

Q *Do I have to read all the Highway Code?*
A Yes, and make sure you understand it. Do
not learn it 'parrot fashion'.

Q *Will I be asked questions which are not
included in the Highway Code?*
A Yes. The examiner, will ask you questions
on all aspects of motoring.

Q *Should I take professional driving lessons?*
A Yes. This is essential because a driving
instructor will be trained to make
observations on your driving that a friend or
relative would probably miss. Many people
do pass the test without professional
lessons, but the observations and remarks
made by a qualified instructor will help you
avoid many pitfalls in future years.

Q *How do I know if my instructor is
competent?*
A The best method is to ask a friend to
recommend one. Failing this, ensure the
instructor you choose displays a badge on
the windscreen to show he is fully qualified.
All approved instructors must pass rigorous
tests before they are allowed to teach. If,
for some reason, you are not happy with
your instructor, change to another one.

Q *How many lessons should I have had before my test?*

A This is a perennial question with no specific answer. It is impossible for anyone to say until you have had some driving experience. As with any skill, some will master it more quickly than others.

Q *How do I know if I am ready for the test?*

A When you and your instructor feel you are driving safely and competently at all times, then you are ready.

Q *Should I take a test for experience?*

A You would be better advised to gain more experience before taking the test. Provided you have had enough practice, there is no reason why you should not pass at the first attempt.

Q *Should I practise in my own car?*

A All driving experience is beneficial and once you have reached a reasonable standard, extra practice helps to build confidence.

Q *Can I remove the head rests?*

A The head 'rests' are in fact head 'restraints' and they are there for a purpose. If, for any reason, you have to stop suddenly they will prevent your head being thrown back. Do not under any circumstances remove them. They are positioned in such a way that they should not interfere with your driving.

Q *What happens if my test is cancelled by the test centre?*

A You will be given another date as soon as one is available.

Q *What happens if I cannot take the test on the appointed day?*

A You are required to give three clear working days' notice. If in any doubt read the appointment card carefully.

Q *What do I do when I arrive at the test centre?*

A Park in a sensible, safe place and go into the waiting room where the examiner will meet you at the appointed time.

2
THE OBJECT
OF THE TEST

Anybody who wishes to drive a car, motorbike or any mechanically propelled vehicle is required by law to take a Department of Transport driving test before they may drive on any road without restriction. This regulation was introduced in 1936. Consequently, anyone who had not obtained a driving licence by that time will have had to take a driving test.

The object of the test is to ensure you have reached a reasonably high standard to enable you to drive on any road without supervision. You will need to satisfy the examiner that you are a competent and safe driver and that you show courtesy and consideration to all other road users. He must be sure you will be able to handle the vehicle you drive in the many and varied situations you are likely to meet on today's busy roads.

The driving examiner is a highly qualified driver who has had to pass rigorous tests of his own driving skills and his ability to notice the faults in others. All examiners are bound by a strict code of conduct. They keep their talking to a minimum and will not chat to you. This is to enable you to concentrate on the job in hand.

During the test you must listen carefully to the examiner's instructions. These will be given clearly and concisely. For example, you will be asked to —
'Move away when ready.'
'Pull in on the left.'
'Take the next road on the right,' and so on.

Do not allow your driving to be affected in any way merely because you are being given directions in a formal manner by a stranger. The examiner's mode of speech is simply to ensure all tests are conducted uniformly. There will be nothing personal in the way he speaks to you.

As you drive, the examiner will be marking any faults as and when you make them. You are not expected to drive faultlessly. Mistakes are divided into three categories —

1   Minor mistakes.
2   Potentially dangerous or serious mistakes.
3   Dangerous mistakes.

Only serious or dangerous mistakes will result in failure.

Driving tests are conducted from Monday to Friday at 9.00, 9.45, 10.45, 11.30, 12.15, 2.00, 2.45, 3.30 and, excluding winter, 4.15.

3
THE TEST REQUIREMENTS

The driving test requirements consist of 20 separate conditions. You will be expected to fulfil all these conditions competently and safely. If you fail your test, you will be given a sheet of paper on which these 20 conditions are laid out and the examiner will underline those on which you failed. Most of the conditions are straightforward, i.e. you either carry them out properly or you do not. But there are others that are open to interpretation. However, as the examiner is looking for a safe and competent drive, it is fairly easy for him to make a decision based on his own driving experience coupled with the prevailing road and weather conditions. We will take each point in turn and describe what is required of you.

1   **Comply with the requirements of the eyesight test**
The examiner will want to be sure your

eyesight is good enough for you to be driving and to this end he will ask you to read a convenient number plate.

The exact requirements are that you can read a number plate from —

(a) 23 metres (75 feet) away if its letters and figures are 9 cm ($3\frac{1}{2}$) in high;
(b) 21 metres (67 feet) away if the letters and figures are 8 cm ($3\frac{1}{8}$ in) high.

This should present no problem but, if you are in any doubt, consult an optician. Should you need glasses or contact lenses, you must wear them at all times when you drive.

2   Know the Highway Code
You will be expected to answer any question the examiner asks you concerning the Highway Code and other motoring matters. Although he is not expecting you to be 100 per cent correct, he will expect you to understand the question and have a general idea. Examples are given later in this book.

3   Take proper precautions before starting the engine
Whenever you start the car you must have the handbrake on and the gear lever in neutral. This usually only happens at the start of the test. However, should you stall

for some reason during the test you must make the car safe by applying the handbrake and selecting neutral before you start the engine again. If you stall on the test, this is only counted as a minor mistake provided you restart the car as described and drive on calmly and safely.

4 **Make proper use of accelerator/clutch/gears/ footbrake/handbrake/steering**
Accelerator — Always use this pedal smoothly. There should be no unnecessary noise or 'racing', so care must be taken when driving under 'clutch control' and you will want to be well practised in this area before you present yourself for examination.
Clutch — The examiner will expect you to have complete control over this pedal. Avoid 'riding the clutch' or jumping your foot off the clutch when changing gear. Do not allow yourself to 'coast' for any distance during the test.
Gears — You are expected to use whichever gear is appropriate at the time and not to stay in a gear too long or change too early. By the time you take the test, gear changes should be positive and smooth. There should be no fear attached to driving in the higher gears.
Footbrake — The footbrake should be used progressively when needed. If you have to brake harshly this will show you have not assessed the situation ahead in enough

time. Good anticipation is vital to good driving.

Handbrake — You must use the handbrake only when it is needed. It must not be used to slow the car down but only to hold the car when stationary.

Steering — There are many faults that arise from improper steering. Firstly, you must ensure you do not cross your hands or let them drop onto your lap. If you do, you could be failed. Secondly, you need to maintain your proper road position at all times. Thirdly, never drive with your hand on the gear lever except when making a gear change.

In all the above points, what is uppermost in the examiner's mind is the smoothness of the drive.

5   **Move away safely/under control**
Safely — To move away safely you must be sure you will not interfere with any other road user. This necessitates careful observation of the road ahead, the mirrors and the blind spots. Special care must be taken to check for pedestrians or cyclists — your examiner will be watching for this.
Under control — You are required to show the examiner that you can drive away on any gradient or angle smoothly. This will be checked specifically when you will be asked to perform a hill start and to move away when pulled in closely behind a parked car.

Correct use of clutch control will be needed to ensure a progressive start.

6   Stop the vehicle in emergency/promptly/under control
You will generally be tested on this in the early stages of the test. It must be done quickly, as you would if a real emergency arose. The examiner will not expect you to allow the car to skid. So this manoeuvre should be practised on both wet and dry roads prior to the test.

7   Reverse into a limited opening either to the right or left under control/with due regard for other road users
This manoeuvre is to show the examiner that you can handle the car in reverse gear. Most people find the reverse difficult simply because they have not had enough practice driving in reverse. You can overcome this by practising more than most! Although the examiner will not expect your reverse to be perfect he will expect it to be reasonably competent.

Under control — You need to keep the car reasonably close to the kerb and make smooth progress. The road you reverse into could be uphill, downhill or flat, and the corner could be sharp or slightly curved. Your practice needs to be on all types of corners.

With due regard for other road users — All other road users will have precedence over you so, should a vehicle approach or a pedestrian wish to cross the road, you will need to wait for them. Keep a lookout, and stop if necessary.

8 **Turn round by means of forward and reverse gears/under control/with due regard for other road users**
The purpose of this exercise is to show the examiner you can manoeuvre your car in a restricted space.
Under control — The examiner will expect you to have complete mastery over the clutch and will want you to judge the size of the road accurately. *Do not hit the kerb*.
With due regard for other road users — As with the reverse, all other road users will have precedence over you. Should a vehicle approach while you are doing this manoeuvre, you must wait and allow it to pass. Should someone signal you to continue, do not simply follow his instruction; take care that the road is clear all round before continuing.

9 **Make effective use of mirror(s) well before signalling/changing direction/slowing down or stopping**
The use of mirrors is of paramount importance when driving. Merely looking in the mirror when you remember is not good enough. What an examiner looks for is 'effective use' of the mirrors. It is vitally important that you know what is around and

behind you at all times and then act on what you see.

Signalling — You need to check carefully every time well before you signal. The examiner will want to be sure that you take notice of what you see and act accordingly. For example, should you be asked to turn right, do not simply follow the instruction. You must ensure no vehicle is coming up to overtake. If there is, then you may need to wait until it has passed before turning.

Changing direction — If you want to overtake another vehicle, to change to another lane or drive round a bend, you will need to check your mirrors first. The examiner will notice if you do not. The side or wing mirrors should be used in conjunction with your internal mirror when necessary.

Slowing down or stopping — When you are approaching a hazard in the road, e.g. a pedestrian crossing, effective use of the mirrors will enable you to time your braking to arrive smoothly at the hazard. Do not forget this; it is extremely important to know what is behind you at all times and how close it is.

The use of the mirrors should have been practised and understood at the early stages of learning so that by the time of the test you are proficient and sure that you can assess the situations quickly.

10 Give signals where necessary/correctly/in good time

Where necessary — Give signals if it will help or warn any other road user, including pedestrians. In the test situation, if you are in any doubt it is better to signal.

Correctly — You must only use signals found in the Highway Code and must never wave anyone on. After an electric indication, you must check the indicator has cancelled when it is no longer needed. Should the indicator cancel before you have completed your manoeuvre, the examiner will expect you to restart it. Conversely, the signal must be cancelled after you have made the manoeuvre.

In good time — A signal needs to be shown early enough for it to be effective. Let the examiner see that you give other road users time to react to your action.

The use of signals covers hand signals as well as indicators. You will not be specifically tested on hand signals but you need to know them. The examiners do not want to see excessive use of the indicators but will penalise you if you do not use them when needed. For example, if you indicate unnecessarily to overtake a parked vehicle, and there is a junction to the right you could be wrongly informing other road users that you intend to turn the corner. In that instance, it would constitute a serious mistake.

11 Take prompt and appropriate action on all traffic signs/road markings/traffic lights/signals given by traffic controllers/other road users
There is a great deal of information on the road and you must be able to assimilate this information and react to it, e.g. should you see a national speed limit sign and the road is clear you will be expected to pick your speed up accordingly. The examiner will not warn you of any given situation but will take note of how you react. The examiner is not there to trap you, he is there to ensure that you handle situations calmly, reasonably and safely.

Traffic signs — The traffic signs are distinctive in their shape, each shape having a specific meaning. Examples are given later in the book and the examiner will expect you to respond to them.

Road markings — All markings painted on the road have a specific purpose too, and you must obey them. As with the signs, there are examples later in the book.

Traffic lights — You must be aware of the difference between traffic lights and Pelican lights and be able to show the examiner that you can act accordingly with each one.

Traffic controllers — In the rare event of the police or a traffic warden directing the traffic, follow their signals as they will take precedence over any signs or road markings.

Other road users — Great care must be taken when reacting to the signals of other road users, e.g. if a pedestrian at a crossing waves you through, be careful there are no other pedestrians about who are acting independently of his signal. When following another vehicle, especially a bus, you need to be aware of the driver's use of indicators. It could mean he intends to turn a corner or pull in to the side. The examiner will be watching to see that you act positively and safely.

12 **Exercise proper care in the use of speed**
Obviously you must always drive at a speed that you can handle. This will vary under different conditions, i.e. if the roads are wet you will need to leave more room to stop. A busy road will need to be negotiated more slowly than an open road. You must, of course, drive within the speed limits at all times.

13 **Make progress by driving at a speed appropriate to the road and traffic conditions/avoiding undue hesitancy**
A common misconception with the test is that, if you drive slowly you won't make mistakes. Unfortunately, the very fact that you are driving slowly is a mistake in itself. The examiner will expect you to have reached a degree of competence that will enable you to keep your driving flowing. If you hesitate at a junction unnecessarily when the road is clear, then the examiner may feel that you are not fitting in with the prevailing road and traffic conditions.

14 Act properly at road junctions
Regulate speed correctly on approach — As
you approach a junction you should arrive
smoothly and safely. The examiner will
expect the correct and controlled use of the
footbrake and gears.
Take effective observation before emerging —
When you arrive at the junction you must
be certain the way is clear before you
commit yourself to entering the road. If you
are in any doubt, pause and check again.
**Position the vehicle correctly before turning
right** — When turning right at a junction,
whether entering or exiting a road, you
must put the car into a position that will
enable you to do it safely and without
hindering other traffic. Take special care of
road markings and parked vehicles. For
further explanation of what is required, turn
to pages 52-4, 74-5 and 89-92.
**Position the vehicle correctly before turning
left** — As with a right turn, care must be
taken to note any road markings and parked
vehicles that may obstruct you. For further
explanation of what is required, see pages
47-9 and 55-6.
Avoid cutting right hand corners — If you
have taken the correct position for a right
turn you should not cut the corner.
However, you may cut the corner if you
turn the wheels too early. If you are not yet
confident about right-hand turns, then give
them more practice. Cutting corners is a
very dangerous thing to do as you will be in

a position where you cannot clearly see any approaching vehicle. A severe view will be taken of this if you do so in your test.

15   Overtake/meet/cross the path of/other vehicles safely

Overtake — There may be occasions on the test when it is necessary to overtake a slower vehicle. The examiner will need to be sure you have assessed the situation in plenty of time. Ensure it is safe to do so, check the traffic all round and signal if necessary. The examiner will be watching to see if you cut in on the vehicle you have overtaken so allow enough room before you return to the left. Extra care must be taken when overtaking cyclists, so leave as much room as is possible to be safe and to show the examiner that you know that this is necessary. If in doubt do not overtake.

Meet — You could find yourself in a narrow road or a road where parked cars make it impossible for two cars to pass. If another vehicle approaches, you will need to look for a safe place to pull over and allow the other vehicle through. It may be easier for the other driver to give way to you but if you are unsure he will, slow down and move over yourself at a convenient place. To enable you to do this, you will need to look as far ahead as possible.

Cross — When turning right into a minor road you must give way to oncoming traffic. This will mean you have to time your arrival at the junction, slowing earlier if necessary. Refer to Chapter 5, section 19, for further explanation.

16 Position the vehicle correctly during normal driving

You need to keep an even position on the road throughout the test. You should not hug the kerb or stray into the middle of the road. As a general rule, one metre from the kerb will be correct. You should practise in a variety of roads to feel confident that you can keep an even distance from any obstruction to the left.

17 Allow adequate clearance to stationary vehicles

When passing parked vehicles, at least one metre must be allowed. Should someone open a door unexpectedly or step out from behind a car, this will leave enough time for both you and them to react. If it is not possible to leave one metre you will need to drive slowly and the examiner will want to see that you are prepared for the unexpected.

18 Take appropriate action at pedestrian crossings

Where pedestrians have precedence, at a Zebra, Pelican or controlled crossing, you must stop for them. By assessing the situation in advance you should not have to brake violently to achieve this. Uppermost in the examiner's mind will be the safety of other road users, especially pedestrians who are very vulnerable.

19 Select a safe position for normal stops
During the test you will be asked to pull in on the left on a number of occasions. Sometimes, you will be told exactly where to pull in and at other times you will be asked to find a convenient place. Try to pull in reasonably soon after you are told but remember that the examiner will expect you to understand that you should not obstruct other road users, i.e. do not park outside a drive, opposite a junction, opposite a car in a narrow road or where it would be illegal to park.

20 Show awareness and anticipation of the actions of pedestrians/cyclists/drivers
Pedestrians — Particular care must be taken with the very young and the very old. As you are driving, be on the lookout for the signs that children may be about, e.g. a child's bike at the side of the road, a football and particularly ice-cream vans. If in doubt, assume there is a pedestrian hidden from view and be ready to stop if necessary.
Cyclists — The majority of us have been cyclists at some time or another and have no doubt cursed the driver who was too close or 'cut us up'. When driving, always keep your distance from a cyclist and if it is unsafe to pass keep back. Assume the cyclist will weave about and wobble and be

ready to act accordingly. When turning left into a road a cyclist may be overtaking you on the inside. You will need to keep a check on cyclists whether in front, at the side or behind you.

Drivers — Other drivers may not be concentrating as hard as you and could do something careless or thoughtless. If you assume all other drivers may not be concentrating you will be ready to react when they do something silly. Over 90 per cent of accidents are caused by human error.

The examiner will want to be sure that you will treat *all* other road users with the courtesy and consideration that you would expect yourself.

It is by assessing your ability on these 20 requirements that the examiner will reach his decision. During the test he carries with him a standardised form on which he marks any mistakes as you make them. An examiner also has other details to complete on this form, such as the prevaling weather conditions, so if you see him making notes it does not necessarily mean you have failed. All mistakes you make, including minor mistakes, must be noted but do remember you will only fail on *dangerous* or *serious mistakes*. Try to concentrate on what you are doing and take no notice of what the examiner is writing.

4
SOME POINTS OF INTEREST

Q *Do I open the door for the examiner?*
A No. He has some details to take concerning the car so will get in after you.

Q *Do I check he has shut his door?*
A You are in full charge of the vehicle so if you are in any doubt ask him to check.

Q *Should I tell him to wear his seat-belt?*
A No. Driving examiners are exempt from wearing them. Most choose to do so, a few may not.

Q *Do I adjust the mirror when I get into the car?*
A There should be no need for this but check you have not nudged it whilst getting in.

Q *If I set my mirror so that I have to move my head to see in it, will this impress the examiner?*

A No. When you look in the mirror you should just have to move your eyes. The examiners are trained to notice eye movements.

Q *Will I drive on a dual-carriageway?*

A This is possible.

Q *Can I drive faster than 30 m.p.h.?*

A You must follow all road signs so if you enter an unrestricted road, i.e. one where the national speed limit applies, and the road is clear then you should pick your speed up accordingly.

Q *Will I be asked to drive up a cul-de-sac?*

A You may use a cul-de-sac to reverse or turn the car round so if you are told to drive up one then do so.

Q *Should I always indicate without exception?*

A It is not necessary if no-one is around but keep a lookout for other road users including pedestrians and people sitting in parked cars. If in doubt, indicate.

Q *Can I let the wheel slide back through my hands?*

A No. Provided you are driving safely there will always be enough time to turn the wheel.

Q *Can I cross my hands?*

A No. The rim of the wheel should be fed through your hands, and you will be penalised if you do not. The reason is that if you need to cross your hands, the examiner will know that you were taking a corner or a bend faster than you could really manage safely.

Q *Should I stop at every junction?*

A You must always stop at STOP signs. At other junctions, be prepared to stop but, if the way is clear, the examiner will expect you to continue.

Q *What if the car rolls back on a hill?*

A By the time of your test you should have complete mastery over the clutch so the situation should not arise. If in doubt, use your handbrake.

Q *Can I use the gears to slow the car?*

A No, you should use the brakes to slow the car and select the correct gear for the speed. Brakes are adequate to cope with anything but the steepest hill. When you brake, the stop lights show up to warn drivers behind you; braking through gears does not produce this warning to others.

Q *Do I have to change gear in strict sequence every time?*

A No. Use whatever gear is necessary for the situation. If you are turning from a main road into a small side road then the examiner will view a move from fourth to second as good driving technique. And if you come up to a STOP sign, to continue straight ahead, then third to first is the simple way.

Q *Do I have to use fourth gear?*
A If you are driving along an open road and have reached the right speed then the examiner will expect you to use fourth gear.

Q *Can I wave someone on?*
A No. You must only use signals that are in the Highway Code. It can be very dangerous to wave someone on.

Q *If someone flashes their lights at me, do I obey?*
A Yes, provided you are sure it is safe to proceed — but keep a good lookout for other road users. Flashing headlights are merely a 'warning of presence'.

Q *Should I flash my lights?*
A It is better not to do so.

Q *Can I sound my horn?*
A Yes, if it is necessary to let someone know you are there — but do not use it as a rebuke.

Q *Should I acknowledge someone if they let me through?*

A Merely nod or smile but do not take your hands off the wheel.

Q *Can I drive through the painted lines marking a bus stop?*

A Yes.

Q *Can I drive through a bus lane?*

A As you approach it there will be a sign informing you of the times it is closed to ordinary traffic. Make sure you allow yourself enough time to read it, because the examiner will expect you to abide by its instructions.

Q *Must the turn in the road be done in three?*

A No. The examiner will ask you to 'turn the car round by means of forward and reverse gears'. So, if the road is a narrow one, it may take five turns. Whatever it takes, do not hit the kerb.

Q *What happens if I think I am going to touch the kerb on the 'reverse'?*

A Stop immediately. Drive forward, straighten the car up and reverse again. Provided you do this carefully, you will not necessarily be failed.

Q *Can I take my seat-belt off for the 'reverse'?*

A Yes, but remember to put it on when moving away again.

Q *Can I stop on the 'reverse'?*
A Yes, as many times as you need to be able to look out for other traffic.

Q *Is the 'reverse' always round a left-hand corner?*
A If you take the test in a van, then you will reverse round a right-hand corner, but for cars a left-hand corner is always used.

Q *What do I do if someone drives down the road into which I am reversing?*
A You must give way to all other road users when you are reversing so you will have to go round and start again.

Q *What if a pedestrian wishes to cross the road behind me when I am reversing?*
A As with other road users you must give way and allow them to cross before continuing with the 'reverse'.

Q *When will I be asked the Highway Code questions?*
A At the end of the actual driving you will be asked to park near the test centre and it is at this stage the examiner will ask you some questions. It could be as many as ten to fifteen.

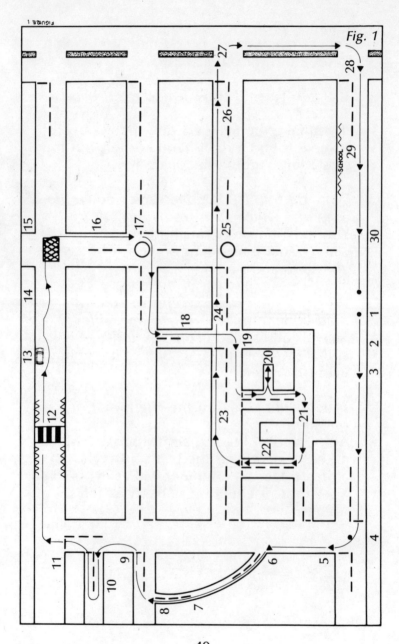

Fig. 1

5
A TYPICAL
TEST ROUTE

The map (Fig. 1) on the previous page includes all the elements you are likely to meet on a test. In this chapter, below each section heading, you will find the test requirements, each designated by the number it was given in Chapter 3. By following the numbers on the map and referring back to Chapter 3, you will be able to see what you need to do and exactly what the examiner is looking for at each point.

1   The examiner will meet you in the waiting room where he will call your name and ask you to sign a form. This is to ensure you are the correct person taking the test, by comparing your signature with the one on your application form. You are not usually asked for your appointment card but have it with you should he need to check. You will then be asked to lead the way to your car.

2 Going to the car

Test requirement: 1

On the way to the car you will be asked
about any disability that may affect your
driving. You will then be asked to read a
number plate, other than your own. When
you arrive at your car the examiner will tell
you to get in while he takes some details of
the car. He will be noting the registration
number, tax disc and the general condition
of the car, including tyres. You should, of
course, have satisfied yourself by now that
the car is fully roadworthy. While he is
checking the car, make yourself
comfortable, put on your seat-belt and
make sure the mirror is properly adjusted.
Once he is in the car he will say to you, 'I
would like you to follow the road ahead
unless I ask you to turn or pull in. Drive on
when you are ready please.'

3   The start

Test requirements: 3, 4, 5, 9, 10, 20

The examiner will be looking for a safe start.
He will be fully aware that you will be
nervous and should you make an ungainly
start will not mark it against you. However,
should you be unsafe, i.e. forget to look
over your shoulder, this will constitute a
serious mistake. At the early stages of
learning to drive you should have formed a
sequence, namely — **Mirror**, **Signal**,
Manoeuvre, and this sequence should be an
automatic action. The sequence follows a
logical pattern —

(a) **Mirror** — including looking around to
be sure all is clear.
(b) **Signal** — to inform all around of your
intentions.
(c) **Manoeuvre** — taking the necessary
action, positively.

You must follow this sequence at all times.
It is not good enough to look in your mirror
after you have signalled as the look in the
mirror is to ensure it is safe to signal
Remember to check your mirror well before
indicating.

When pulling away from the side of the road it is extremely important to check over your shoulder. Also check any places you cannot see in your mirrors.

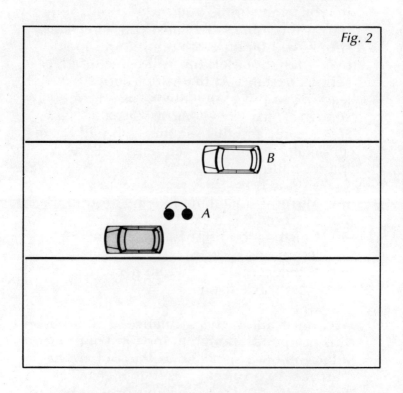

Fig. 2

If there is a cyclist at **A** or a parked car at **B** (Figure 2), you would not be able to see either in your mirrors.

Following the start you will drive for a minute or two to allow you to relax.

4   A mini-roundabout

Test requirements: 4, 9, 10, 14, 15, 20

As you approach the roundabout the
examiner will inform you in plenty of time
that he wishes you to turn right.
Remembering your **M**, **S**, **M** routine, take up
a safe position. Approach the roundabout in
second gear and, if you are able to see the
road to the right is clear, then proceed
steadily round. Should a vehicle be
approaching from the right, you must give
way to it. If the area is small you may drive
over the paint on the road.

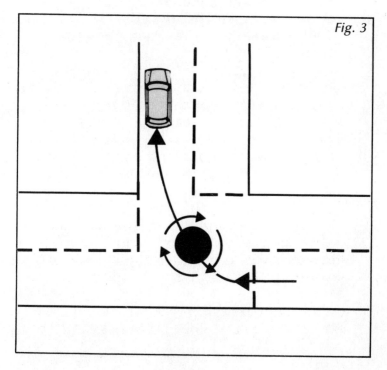

Fig. 3

5   The 'emergency stop'

Test requirements: 5, 6

You will be asked to pull in to the left and the examiner will then inform you of what he requires and the signal he will give when he wants you to stop. As you pull away, build up your speed steadily as you would under ordinary circumstances. When he gives you the signal, brake firmly and at the last second, press down the clutch to stop the car stalling.

If you skid, it will be because you have stamped on the brake. Should this happen, release the brake and immediately try again. At all costs keep the car straight on the road. The examiner wants to see a quick but controlled stop; he will not be impressed if you slam to a stop and the car slides. This exercise needs to be practised from the early stages of your learning, so you always know how to react if a real emergency should arise. Do not worry about the wear on your brakes; safety must always come before economy when driving. Once you have stopped, put the handbrake on and the gear lever into neutral. You will then be asked to drive away when ready; as you drive on, check for other traffic, looking over both shoulders and in your mirror.

6   Left turn in

Test requirements: 4, 9, 10, 14, 20

As you approach the junction, assess the
situation. Here we have a left turn into a
narrow road. Should a car be driving
towards you in the road he may be on your
side, so you will need to take the corner
slowly enough to be able to cope with this.
Any pedestrians crossing the road have
precedence, so allow them to cross,
stopping if necessary.
A general rule with corners is:
   First gear leaving
   Second gear entering
Following this rule will give you enough
time to check for traffic. Do not do
otherwise unless the roads and your view of
them are obviously clear.

The shape of junctions vary and you will be
expected to deal with each junction as it is.
Fig. 4 shows three possible situations you
may meet.

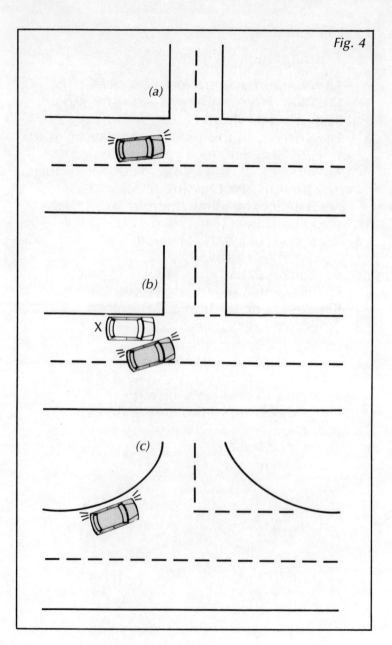

(a) Turning into a narrow road means you need to give yourself more time, so take the corner slowly.

(b) On today's busy roads, a corner where there are no obstructions is the exception rather than the rule. Should a car be parked near the corner at **X** you may need to take the corner wider to avoid it.

(c) More of a bend than a corner, so your car should follow the bend in the road. If all is clear it may be possible to take a corner like this in third gear.

7   A narrow road with a bend

Test requirements: 9, 12, 15, 17, 20

You will need to check well ahead and, should a car approach from the other direction, find a convenient place to pull in. With the bend in the road, ensure you stay on the left at all times, if possible.

With the car approaching, as in Fig. 5, you have a choice of two places to pull into. If you can slow down in enough time, wait at **A** but do not rush yourself because if necessary you could always move into **B** while the other car waits opposite.

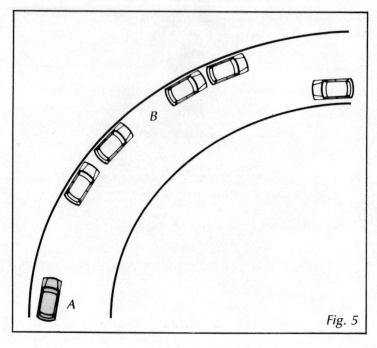

Fig. 5

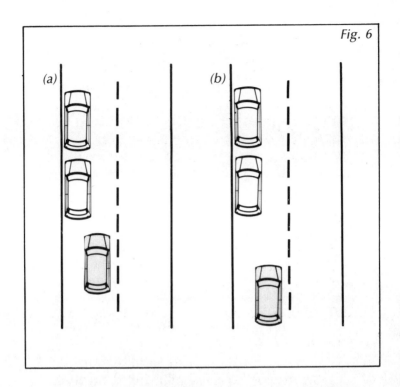

Fig. 6

When giving way to a vehicle from the opposite direction, always slow the car down before moving over as this will give you enough time to take up a good position.

In Fig. 6 **(a)**, the driver has made it very difficult to drive on by getting too close to the parked car.

In Fig. 6 **(b)**, the car is out of the way enough to let an opposing vehicle through but has still left sufficient room to drive on comfortably.

8 Right turn out

Test requirements: 4, 9, 10, 14, 20

As you approach the end of the road be sure you take up a position well to the left to enable another vehicle to turn into the road. As you need to give way you will require first gear, but, should the road be clear, you do not need to stop. However, if you are unsure then do stop and check again.

Fig. 7 shows three possible situations you may meet when making a right-hand turn out.

(a) With a narrow road, the car needs to be positioned well to the left.
(b) At an ordinary junction you should be just left of the centre of the road. If there are no road markings you must judge where the centre line would be.
(c) In this diagram the parked car makes the road narrow and so you will need to keep to the left leaving enough room for a vehicle turning in.

In all cases, your wheels should be straight at the end of the road and you should only start turning them as you emerge.

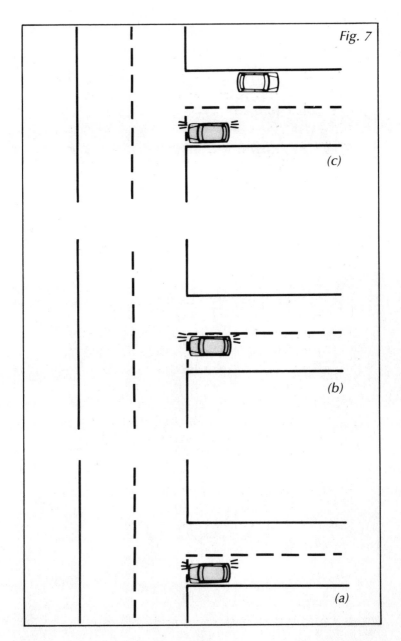

Fig. 7

(c)

(b)

(a)

53

Turning right out of a road is where the majority of accidents, in towns, happen. If there are parked cars or other obstructions blocking your view, as in Fig. 8, you must creep slowly out to a point where you can see clearly both ways. If a vehicle comes towards you, give way. Some may stop to let you out but others will drive round.

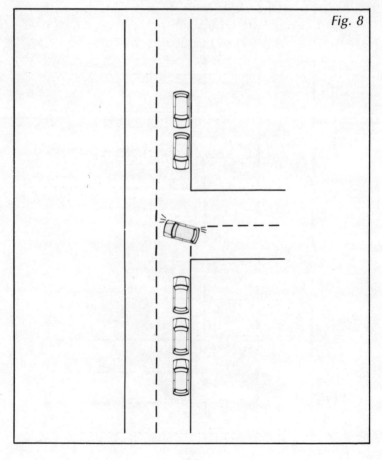

Fig. 8

9   Left turn out

Test requirements: 4, 9, 10, 14, 20

As you arrive at the end of the road the examiner will be looking for a smooth and regulated approach (see Fig. 9). If all is clear, you should be able to slip into first gear while looking for traffic. Provided that you have looked right, left and right again and you are sure it is safe to move out without impeding anyone (including pedestrians) then you need not stop. As mentioned earlier, you may be able to drive

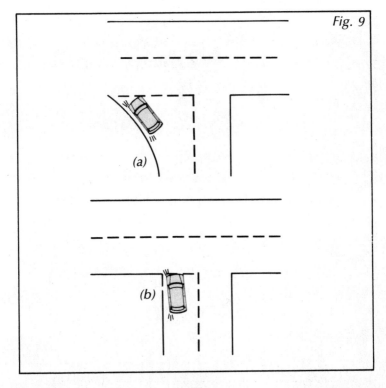

Fig. 9

(a)

(b)

on in second gear but if you are in any doubt use first. Always keep a careful look out for cyclists.

(a) You will need to tuck into the corner and follow the bend round.
(b) As you arrive at the junction, keep the car about 45 centimetres from the kerb and turn the wheels ready to emerge on the left-hand side of the main road.

10   Turn in the road

Test requirement: 8

For the 'turn in the road', you will be asked
to pull into the side of the road where the
examiner will explain what he requires. He
will say to you: 'Turn the car around by
means of forward and reverse gears. Try not
to hit the kerb.'

Although it is usually possible to do this
exercise in three movements, on a narrow
road it may take five. Provided you do not
hit the kerb and you keep the car under
control at all times, it does not matter how
many moves you take. (See Fig. 10.)

(a) When you are sure the road is clear,
    drive slowly to the other side, turning
    the wheel quickly to the right. About
    one metre from the kerb, turn the
    wheel back to the left, as much as you
    can, ready for the next stage.
(b) Stop and apply the handbrake, then
    checking carefully for traffic and being
    prepared to wait, select reverse gear.
    Reverse slowly back, turning the wheel
    quickly to the left. Approximately one
    metre from the kerb, turn the wheel
    back to the right ready to drive on.
(c) Stop and apply the handbrake. Check
    for traffic and select first gear. If all is
    clear, drive on without touching the
    kerb.

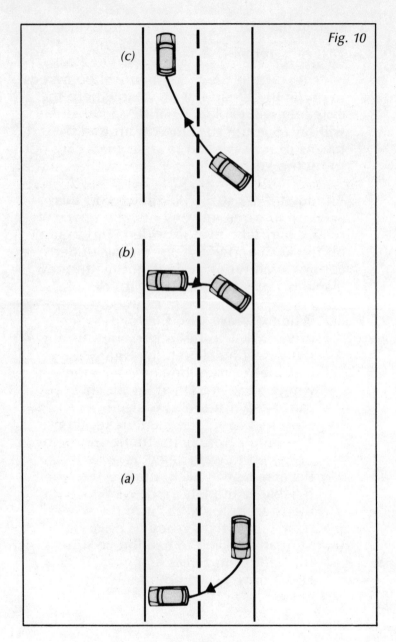

The examiner will not choose a busy road to do the 'turn in the road', but should another vehicle come along you must allow it to pass. Should a vehicle wait for you, do not allow the driver to put you off; just concentrate on the job in hand. Extra care must be taken for cyclists as they can pass where there isn't enough room for a car. This is one of the few occasions where you may take your seat-belt off, but it is not advisable as you will continue driving when you have finished and will not pull into the left again.

You do not need to indicate at the start of the 'turn in the road' as you should only be doing this manoeuvre if you are sure the road is completely clear.

This manoeuvre is included in the driving test to show your ability to control the car in a restricted space. The next time you put this exercise into practice could be in a busy car park where the equivalent of the kerbs would be other cars, hence the importance of not hitting the kerbs. The examiner cannot be expected to pass you if you are likely to cause mayhem the next time you go shopping.

11 STOP sign

Test requirements: 4, 9, 10, 11, 14, 20

It is most important that you realise you have arrived at a STOP sign and not an ordinary 'Give Way'. The signs are very distinctive and you will be failed if you do not stop. This should make things easier as you can concentrate solely on your position and not worry whether the road is clear enough for you to continue. Unless the road is on a hill, there is generally no need to use the handbrake.

12 Zebra crossing

Test requirements: 4, 9, 11, 18, 20

The examiner will expect you to notice the crossing well in advance and act accordingly. As you approach, keep a careful look out for any pedestrians near the crossing, taking special care if children are about as they may rush out without looking. At a Zebra crossing, pedestrians have precedence once they put their foot on the actual crossing. However, if they are waiting at the side you should stop for them. If a 'helpful' pedestrian waves you on, first take great care to check that there is no-one else around.

13 Moving off at an angle

Test requirements: 4, 5, 9, 10, 17, 20

The examiner will ask you to pull into the
left, reasonably close to the car in front, and
then to drive on again. This is a situation
you will meet many times in your life and
the examiner must be sure you are able to
perform it safely. He will want to see good
clutch control and careful observation and
signalling. (See Fig. 11.)

(a) This is how the manoeuvre should be
     performed.
(b) This shows you have tried to do it too
     fast and have not used the clutch to full
     effect.

Although you must, obviously, practise this
manoeuvre prior to the test, it is wise to
leave it until you are happy with your use of
the clutch before you use somebody else's
car. Incorrect use of the clutch could be
very unfortunate.

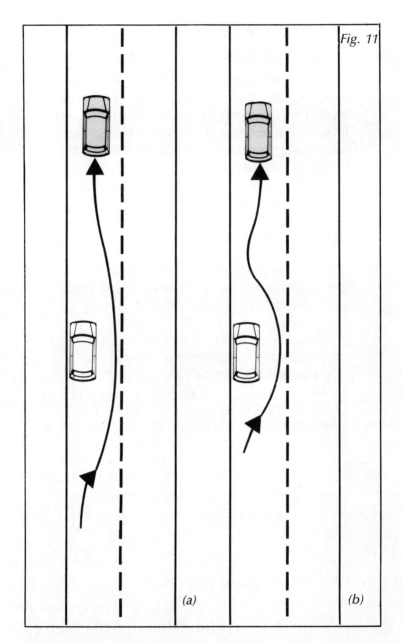

(a)   *(b)*

63

14 Overtaking

Test requirements: 4, 9, 10, 13, 15, 16, 20

Should you find yourself behind a slow vehicle, e.g. a milk float, and it is safe to overtake, you will be expected to do so. Ensure you check all around (using the mirror-signal-manoeuvre sequence) in enough time to be able to move out smoothly. An indicator will warn everybody, including the driver, that you are overtaking so it should always be used on occasions like this. (See Fig. 12.)

(a) This is how the action should be performed. You should cancel your indicator at **X**.
(b) Here the driver of the vehicle overtaking has allowed himself to get too close and then, when he has passed, has moved back in too early.

Overtaking is always a dangerous manoeuvre, as you have to be on the other side of the road. In the Highway Code there are lots of occasions where you are told not to overtake. Always check it is safe and legal to do so before you commit yourself and, if you are at all unsure, hang back and wait.

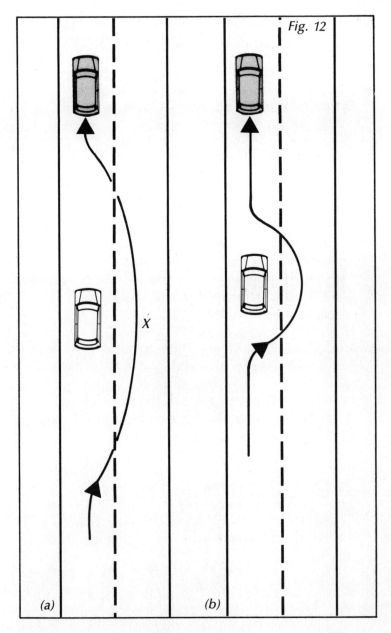

Fig. 12

(a)   (b)

15 Traffic lights with a box junction

Test requirements: 4, 9, 10, 11, 14, 20

Although there will be a lot of information to take in here, provided you know and understand the Highway Code, it should provide no problem.

Take it step by step. If the lights are green and the road to the right is clear (i.e. your exit from the box is not blocked) drive into the box and wait for oncoming traffic. Should the lights change back to red while you are waiting in the box, you must drive on when it is safe as you would hinder traffic by staying put. If the lights are red or the road to the right is not clear, wait behind the line. (See Fig. 13.)

(a) Wait here if the lights are red or the exit road is blocked.
(b) Wait here if the lights are green but traffic is approaching from the road opposite and your exit from the box is clear.

The rules of a box junction state: 'Do not enter the box unless your exit road is clear.' In Fig. 13, the exit road is marked. As the road is clear, by obeying the rule you may enter the box and wait for oncoming traffic.

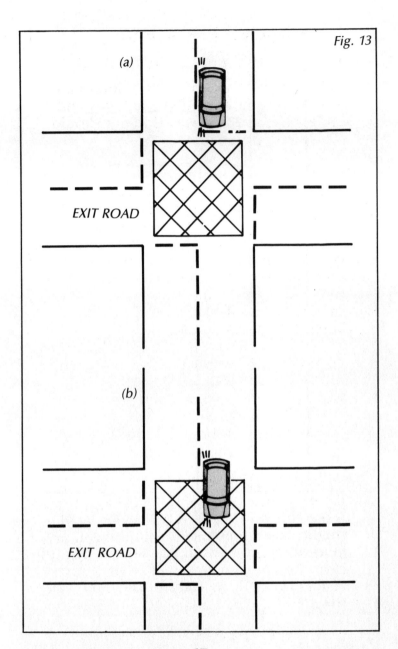

Fig. 13

(a)

EXIT ROAD

(b)

EXIT ROAD

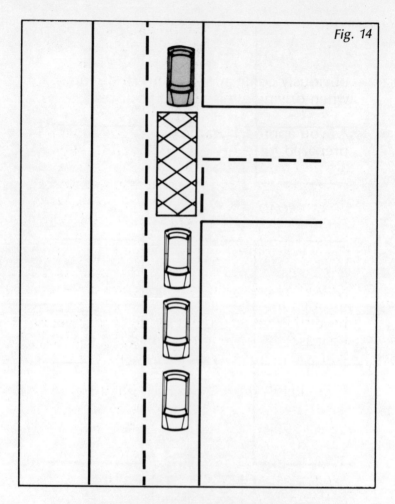

Fig. 14

A box junction merely emphasises what should be common sense: to leave a junction clear. If, as in Fig. 14, you cannot clear the junction, you must wait before it and allow traffic to enter or leave the side road.

Although we only have one set of traffic lights on our imaginary test, you may well meet more on your test, and you will obviously come across them all the time when driving after passing your test.

As you approach traffic lights, you must be prepared for every eventuality. If the lights are green when you first see them, they could change back to red as you get closer — so check your mirror and be prepared to stop. This does not mean you should slow down or change gear unnecessarily. If necessary, you can stop in any gear. If the lights change when you are too close to stop in a controlled manner, then drive through the amber light. If you find you have to drive through a red light this will be because you have approached too fast and you will be penalised accordingly.

If the lights are red when you first see them, be prepared for a change to green, if necessary by changing from fourth to second gear.

When waiting at red lights, use the handbrake. Excessive use of clutch control harms the engine and, should your foot slip, it could be very dangerous. You have plenty of time to prepare when the lights change as you must not move until they change to green. Red and amber lights together mean 'stop'.

16   A busy road

Test requirements: 11, 12, 16, 17, 20

In a busy road there will be more things to look out for so your speed will need to be slow enough to enable you to take in all that is happening. There are numerous situations that could arise. A child could run out between parked cars, a driver could pull out without looking, etc. Obviously things such as these could happen anywhere but, where there are more people about, the likelihood of them happening is greater. Being an experienced driver, the examiner will be aware of what is happening but you, of course, cannot rely on him to help. If the car you are driving is not fitted with dual controls he may not be able to do so. In any event, by the time you go for your test you should be able to deal with situations such as these.

17 Right turn at a roundabout

Test requirements: 4, 9, 10, 11, 13, 14, 15, 20

The purpose of a roundabout is to keep
traffic flowing, so you will be expected to
continue on if the way is clear. The
examiner will inform you in plenty of time
as to which exit he wishes you to take off a
roundabout. As you are turning right this
time, you will need to move safely over to
the centre of the road as you approach. By
changing down to second gear, two to three
car lengths away from the entrance, you
should allow yourself enough time to check
to the right and, if all is clear, continue.

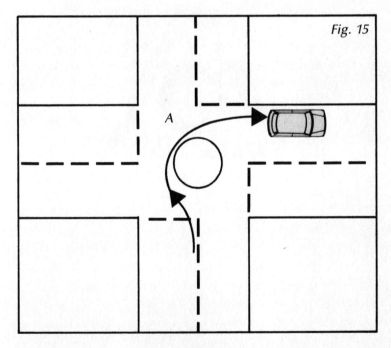

Fig. 15

As seen in Fig. 15, you should stay close to the centre of the roundabout and, as you come off, move to the left.
Indicate right as you drive onto the roundabout and then flick your indicator to the left at **A**, having first checked your mirror.

Although roundabouts vary in shape and the number of exits, the rule to follow is straightforward — give way to the right. Before taking your test, you will need to practise on various roundabouts so that even the busy ones hold no fear for you.

18 The 'hill start'

Test requirements: 5, 9, 10, 19

At some stage of your test, you will be asked to pull in on a hill to show the examiner you can drive off on a gradient. It is imperative you do not roll back on this manoeuvre. You should be able to coordinate the clutch and accelerator pedals well enough to be able to hold the car stationary when the handbrake is released. Every time you pull out from the side of the road you need careful observation and correct signalling. If you are unhappy with your ability to control the pedals, you may find you jump away and don't leave enough time for checking your blind spots.

The correct order to do this exercise is as follows:
(1) Select first gear.
(2) Check the mirror. If it is not clear — wait.
(3) When it is clear, find the biting point and release the handbrake. Hold the car stationary.
(4) Check the mirror again and indicate.
(5) Look over your shoulder and drive away.

If you follow the above procedure, you will not have to hold the car for too long at the biting point and so will not put too much wear and tear on the clutch plates — and your nerves.

19 Right turn in

Test requirements: 4, 9, 10, 14, 15, 20

When turning right into a side road, you must signal your intentions early enough to warn any vehicles behind not to attempt to overtake. If you have to wait for traffic approaching, take up a position with the front of the car opposite the middle of the road you wish to turn into. If there is no traffic approaching, take care when you turn that no pedestrians are crossing the road into which you are turning. (See Fig. 16.) Do not cut the corner.

(a) If the road is clear enough, this is the position you should take before turning.

(b) If there are parked cars or an obstruction near the corner, ensure you leave enough room for approaching vehicles to drive through.

Approaching a right turn, if traffic allows it, try to time your arrival so that you can continue without stopping. If there is an oncoming vehicle travelling at such a speed that it will arrive at the junction at the same time as you, slow down a little earlier and turn behind it. Do not race to the junction in order to beat it. You will be failed for not 'crossing the path of other vehicles safely'.

Any vehicles turning right out of the side road should give you priority.

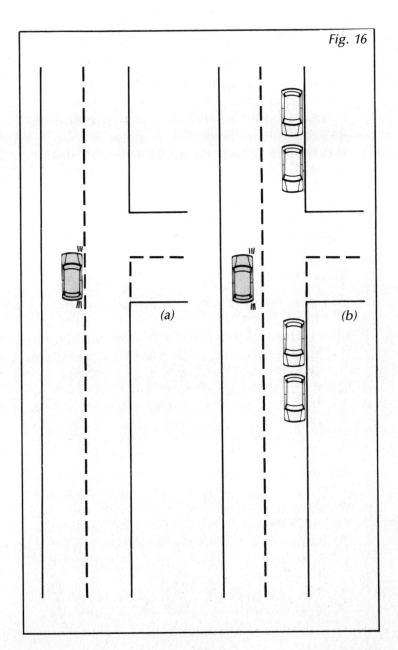

20 The reverse

Test requirement: 7

This is the part of the test that most candidates fear. The most usual reason for failure on the 'reverse' is simply not enough practice beforehand. If you enter for the test feeling uncertain about any part of it, you are going to rely on luck and cannot expect to pass. The 'reverse' does require lots of practice and, though it is not an easy manoeuvre, it is, however, extremely important. You cannot expect the examiner to pass you if you cannot drive competently in *all* gears. (See Fig. 17.)

(1) The examiner will ask you to pull into the left before the road and explain what he wants you to do. As you drive past the road, check the gradient and the angle of the corner.

(2) Drive into a position about three car lengths from the corner, keeping about 45 centimetres from the kerb. Check all round for traffic and then reverse slowly back.

(3) When you reach the corner, stop, check all round for traffic and, if clear, turn the wheel smoothly to the left while keeping the car moving slowly.

(4) When you get to a position parallel to the kerb, turn the wheel smoothly back to straighten the vehicle.

(5) Reverse back until the examiner tells you to stop.

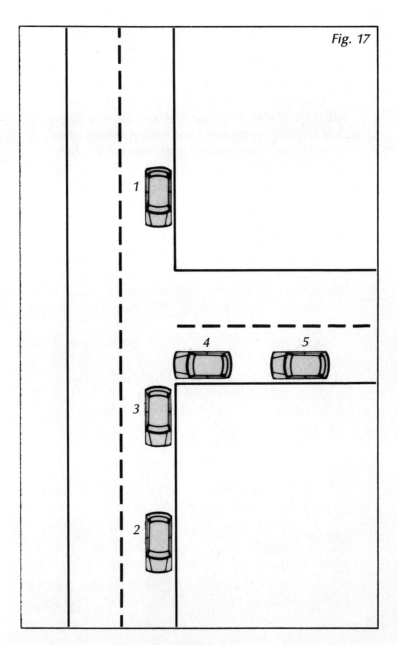

If you think of the reverse as a sequence of actions, as above, and take each one in turn, it should pass off smoothly.

Should it go slightly wrong and you swing wide or drive into the kerb, you do not automatically fail. If you swing wide, move slowly back into the kerb; do not rush yourself as you may then hit it. If you turn too tightly and feel that you are going to hit the kerb, stop immediately, use first gear and drive forward to straighten up, then reverse back again when safe. There is no need to start the whole manoeuvre again.

The observation on the 'reverse' is of paramount importance. All other road users have precedence over you, so if any are around you must wait for them to pass. If a vehicle drives down the road you are reversing into, you will need to drive around the corner and start again. Unless you are driving a very old car, when you put the gear lever into reverse, white lights shine at the back of the car to warn other road users. However, do not assume everybody knows this and, if necessary, move out of the way.

Obviously, not all corners are the same. If the corner you meet is as in Fig. 18 (a), full lock on the wheel will be needed to ensure you do not swing wide. If the corner is the same as Fig. 18 (b), you will need to follow the kerb by turning the wheel slowly.

You may take your seat-belt off for the reverse but do not forget to put it back on before driving on.

The major point with the 'reverse' is *practice*.

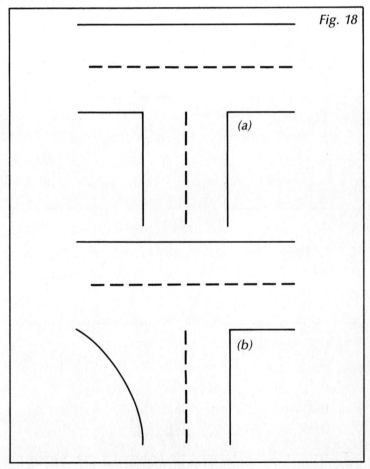

Fig. 18

21   Unmarked Crossroads

Test requirements: 4, 9, 12, 14, 20

You will find that road markings are not painted at the ends of every road. It would be prohibitively expensive to do this. Where there are no markings, it is usually because the right of way is obvious. However, there are occasions where the right of way is not obvious, but still there are no markings. This may be because the road has recently been resurfaced or simply the paint has worn out and not been replaced.

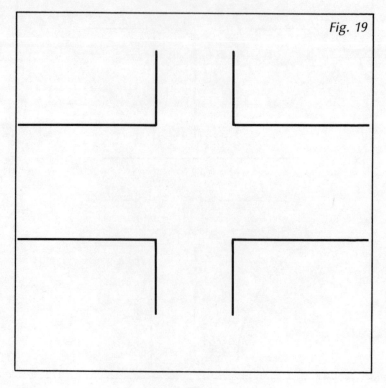

Fig. 19

In Fig. 19, you would assume that the larger road is the main road and you would have priority driving along it. This is not necessarily true. If there are no markings or signs to indicate otherwise, both roads at an unmarked crossroads have equal priority.

As you approach any crossroads, even those with road markings, you must check both side roads as you cannot assume all other drivers will behave as they should. If you are in any doubt as to who has priority, assume you do not and be prepared to give way.

22 One-way street

Test requirements: 9, 10, 11, 14, 16, 20

It is very likely you will meet either a
one-way street or a one-way system on your
test. The examiner will not inform you it is a
one-way street but will expect you to notice.

Fig. 20 (a) shows the correct way to enter a
one-way street. You will not fail if you enter
the road as in Fig. 20 (b), but it is not
correct.

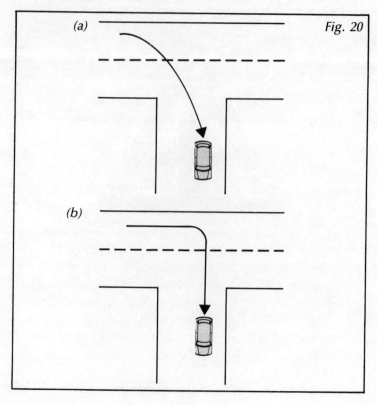

Fig. 20

If, as in our test route, you need to turn right at the end of the road, you must move to the right-hand side of the road as early as possible. Your exit position should be as in Fig. 21.

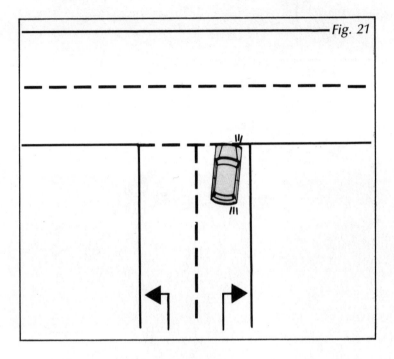

Fig. 21

One-way systems have become increasingly popular in towns and cities as they cut down on traffic congestion by making everybody flow round in the same direction. There are always plenty of signs to inform you which lane to take and you will need to pay attention to these as the examiner may ask you to follow a certain sign.

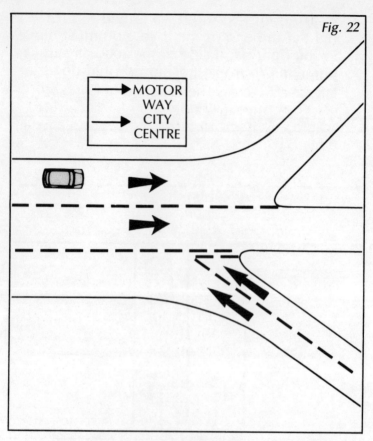

Fig. 22

MOTOR
WAY
CITY
CENTRE

In Fig. 22, if you are asked to follow the signs to the city centre, you will need to move into the right-hand lane and stay in that lane until you see another sign or the examiner gives you further directions.

It pays to familiarise yourself with any awkward one-way systems in the vicinity of the test centre prior to your actual test.

23 Downhill start

Test requirements: 4, 5, 9, 10, 19, 20

You will not necessarily do a particular exercise to show the examiner a downhill start but there will doubtless be occasions where you need to move away when facing downhill.

It is imperative that you retain full control over the car at all times. Therefore, the procedure should be as follows:

(1) Select gear, usually first, but if the road is steep enough use second gear to start.

(2) Hold the car with the footbrake and release the handbrake.

(3) Check the mirrors and indicate if clear.

(4) Look over your shoulder.

(5) Take your foot off the brake and move it over to the accelerator as you let the clutch up. Steer out into the road.

If you start in this way, the car will not rush off down the hill and you will have both hands on the wheel to do any steering that is necessary.

24 Straight across a junction

Test requirements: 4, 9, 11, 14, 15, 20

At the beginning of the test the examiner
has asked you to follow the road unless told
to turn. Should you approach a junction at
which he wishes you to continue straight
ahead, he will say nothing. This is to make
sure you notice the junction.

As you approach, treat it the same as any
junction and slow down in plenty of time.
Keep looking right, left and right as you
cross. (See Fig. 23.) If there is a STOP sign
you will, of course, be expected to stop.

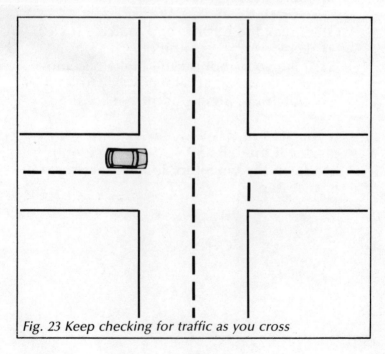

Fig. 23 Keep checking for traffic as you cross

25 Straight ahead at a roundabout

Test requirements: 4, 9, 10, 11, 13, 14, 15, 20

See Fig. 24. As you approach the roundabout, stay to the left and keep to the left as you drive round the roundabout. As with the right turn, you should continue in second gear if the way is clear.

You must indicate left at **X** to inform other road users you intend to leave the roundabout.

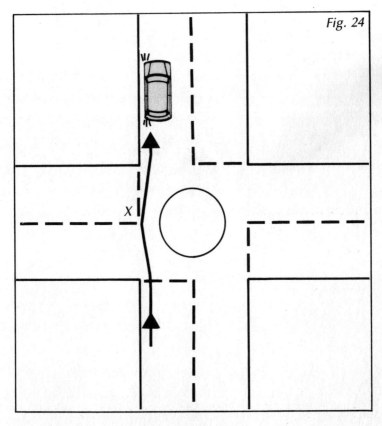

Fig. 24

26 Pelican crossing

Test requirements: 9, 11, 12, 18, 20

The rules of a Pelican crossing are:
(1) Red — stop.
(2) Amber — stop.
(3) Amber flashing — give way to
pedestrians.
(4) Green — proceed if clear.

When the amber light is flashing, do not rev
your engine to hurry pedestrians along.
Wait until they have completely crossed and
check for any that hurry on to the road
trying to beat the lights.

27 Right turn onto a dual-carriageway

Test requirements: 4, 9, 10, 11, 14, 15, 20

Traffic will be travelling faster on a dual-carriageway, therefore you will need to look further along the road to be certain it is safe to enter.

There are two ways of joining a dual-carriageway. How you tackle it will depend on the way the central reservation is laid out.

In Fig. 25 (a), there is not enough room for a car to wait in the middle and so the road must be clear both ways before you enter.

In Fig. 25 (b), there is enough space to wait in the middle and here you should treat the dual-carriageway as two separate roads. Cross the first side and wait in the centre for the opposite side to be clear.

In both cases, as you join the dual-carriageway you should drive into the left-hand lane, leaving the right-hand lane clear for traffic to overtake.

Once on the dual-carriageway, if the signs and conditions dictate, you may be able to drive faster than 30 m.p.h.

Fig. 25

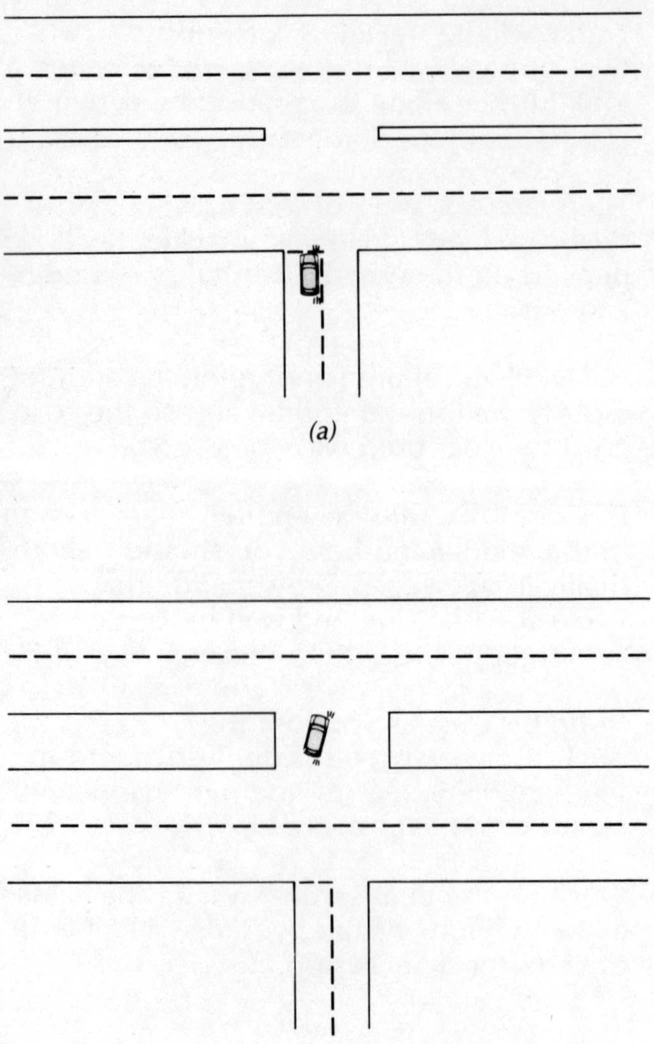

(a)

(b)

28 Turning right off a dual-carriageway

Test requirements: 4, 9, 10, 11, 12, 13, 14, 15, 16, 20

See Fig. 26. When you are asked to turn right, act promptly as the traffic will be moving fast. Check the mirror and signal. If a car is overtaking, wait until it has passed, check your side mirror and blind spot and move smoothly into the right-hand lane. Drive into the gap in the central reservation, following any road markings there may be.

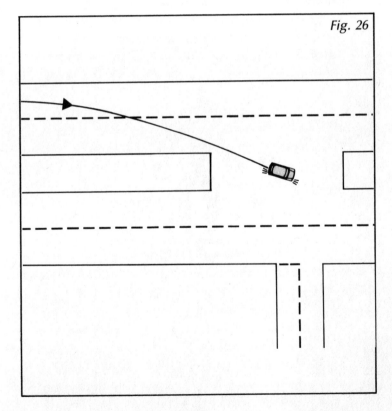

Fig. 26

When the opposite carriageway is clear, steer smoothly across into the side road. The examiner will want to see the whole manoeuvre accomplished calmly, so ensure you take it at a speed that will enable you to cope without hindering other road users.

A dual-carriageway will not necessarily be included in your test, but you must feel confident in your ability to deal with them anyway. A lot of drivers tend to pick their speed up rapidly as they enter a dual-carriageway and there are more accidents to drivers on them than anywhere else. So always take great care when entering or leaving one.

29 A school

Test requirements: 9, 11, 12, 18, 20

Taking a test in an urban area generally involves passing a school somewhere. If it is when the children should be in classes, do not assume they all will be. At the beginning and end of the school day, a crossing patrol could be in operation. Always obey the traffic controller and keep a lookout for any children crossing the road nearby or running into the road.

Most pedestrian fatalities happen to older people and children. Their actions are very unpredictable so extra care must be taken when you see them.

30 The Highway Code

Test requirement: 2

You will be asked to pull in to the left and park reasonably close to the test centre. When you have parked, make sure the car is safe, i.e. handbrake on and gear lever in neutral, before switching the engine off. Take your seat-belt off and relax.

Here the examiner will ask you some questions (see Chapter 6), and then he will inform you of the result.

The driving test is quite concentrated as the examiners have only approximately 30 minutes to make a decision and must be sure you can fulfil all the requirements in that time. When you have passed you are unlikely to meet all the hazards of a test in any one day but at some time or another you will meet them all.

Provided you have practised enough before the test, you should not find it too difficult. If you concentrate, look well ahead and give yourself time to react, everything should go smoothly. The examiners take no pleasure in failing you, but if you are not competent it would be unsafe for them to allow you on the road.

By the time you take the test, you should have satisfied yourself that you can cope safely with all the situations above. If you cannot truthfully answer 'yes', then you will need some luck to pass on the day. Luck has a tendency to desert us when we need it most!

The Highway Code

HMSO 60p net

6
HIGHWAY CODE QUESTIONS

The Highway Code questions at the end of the test are designed to show the examiner you have a knowledge of motoring over and above what you have shown him in your driving.

In some other countries learner drivers are required to pass a written test before they are allowed to take the driving test. As this regulation is not in force in this country, we make do with a verbal test at the end of the drive.

It is in your own best interest to learn as much about motoring as you can prior to the test as, having passed the test, sadly very few people ever pick up a Highway Code booklet again. The more you learn and understand now, the safer you will be in the future.

What follows are merely examples of the type of questions you may be asked. It is unlikely it will be good enough for you to learn these and nothing else. The best method of tackling this section of the book would be to study the Highway Code before reading the questions and then see how many you can answer yourself.

QUESTIONS ON EVERYDAY SITUATIONS

Q *What should you pay particular attention to before using your car on a highway?*

A The overall condition of the car, in particular lights, brakes, windscreen wipers and tyres.

Q *What must you ensure concerning your tyres?*

A That they have enough tread depth (1 mm all round), that they are properly inflated and that they are free from cuts and other defects.

Q *At what age must a car have an M.O.T. certificate?*

A Three years.

Q *What is the speed limit in a built-up area?*

A 30 m.p.h.

Q *What follows RED at Traffic lights?*
A RED and AMBER.

Q *What follows RED at pelican lights?*
A AMBER flashing on and off.

Q *What does the flashing AMBER light mean?*
A You may proceed but should give way to any pedestrians already on the crossing.

Q *What are the overall stopping distances?*

A

M.p.h.	Metres	Feet
20	12	40
30	23	75
40	36	120
50	53	175
60	73	240
70	96	315

Q *What is meant by the above answer?*
A These are the distances it would take to stop the car completely on a dry road with good brakes and tyres from the moment a hazard is seen. It combines 'thinking' and 'braking' time.

Q *Will this change if the roads are wet?*
A Yes, you will need at least to double the distance when wet.

Q *What is the 'two second rule'?*

A This is the minimum distance you should leave between you and the vehicle in front under normal conditions to enable you to stop safely.

Q *What are the regulations concerning the use of the horn?*

A The horn must not be used between the hours of 11.30 p.m. and 7.00 a.m. in a built-up area, or when the car is stationary. It should **never** be used as a rebuke.

Q *What is the meaning of flashing headlamps?*

A This is merely a warning of presence to let other road users know you are there.

Q *What are you not allowed to do in the area marked by zigzag lines at a zebra crossing?*

A Park or overtake.

Q *What is the purpose of a central reservation on a zebra crossing?*

A This divides the crossing into two separate sections and you only need give way to any pedestrians on your side.

Q *Where **must** you **not** overtake?*

A 1 If you would have to cross or straddle double white lines with a solid line nearest you.

    2 Within the zigzag area at a zebra crossing.

    3 After a 'No Overtaking' sign.

Q *Where is it also advisable not to overtake?*
A 1   On the brow of a hill.
     2   On a hump backed bridge.
     3   Where the road narrows.
     4   On a level crossing.
     5   On a corner or bend.
     6   At a road junction.
     7   Where, by overtaking, another vehicle would be endangered.
     8   On areas marked with diagonal stripes or chevrons.

Q *What is the last thing you must do before pulling away from the side of the road?*
A Check over your shoulder for anything hidden in your blind spot.

Q *How would you inform a pedestrian at a crossing that you intend to slow down and allow him to cross?*
A By using a hand signal — arm extended out of window and raised and lowered gently.

Q *If you cannot see clearly behind when reversing, what should you do?*
A Ask someone to guide you.

Q *If someone is reversing into your path, what would be your first action?*
A Toot the horn as a warning of your presence.

Q *What lights should you put on at dusk?*
A Dipped headlights.

Q *What rules must you follow when you park at night?*

A Park on the left, not closer than 15 metres to a junction, and leave some lights on if it is not a built-up area.

Q *Where may you overtake a vehicle on the left?*

A 1 When the driver in front is turning right.
2 When turning left.
3 When traffic is moving slowly in lanes.
4 In a one-way street.

Q *What extra precautions should you take when parking on a hill?*

A Leave the car in gear — first uphill and reverse downhill — and turn the wheels into the kerb downhill and away from the kerb uphill.

Q *What distance should you keep when driving past parked cars?*

A At least one metre, to allow enough room if a driver opens a door unexpectedly.

Q *What steps would you take to prevent theft?*

A 1 Remove the key
2 Lock valuables in the boot.
3 Lock doors and secure windows.
4 Use an alarm.

QUESTIONS ON UNUSUAL SITUATIONS

Q *How would you tell if a pedestrian is blind and deaf?*

A He would be carrying a white stick with two red reflectorised bands around it.

Q *What should be your action when driving past animals?*

A Drive slowly, do not rev engine, do not toot the horn.

Q *What action should you take if an emergency vehicle, i.e. police car, ambulance or fire engine, approaches from behind with its siren on?*

A Move out of the way as quickly as possible. You do not necessarily have to stop, but ensure you leave enough room for it to drive through without hindrance.

Q *On a single track road with a gradient, who should give way if two vehicles meet?*

A The vehicle coming downhill.

Q *What are the rules for 'common land'?*

A You must not park more than 15 metres from the road.

Q *What is the 'fog code'?*

A Slow down, use headlights, windscreen wipers and fog lights. Do not hang on to the tail lights of the car in front.

Q *What is the speed limit on a dual-carriageway?*

A 70 m.p.h. unless otherwise stated.

Q *What are the main causes of skids?*

A Harsh braking, harsh acceleration, harsh cornering, bald tyres, or any combination of these.

Q *If, in a skid, the rear of your car moves to the right, which way should you steer?*

A To the right to keep the car straight on the road.

Q *With what should you be concerned after driving through flood water?*

A The brakes. You should gently test them to ensure no water has stayed in there.

Q *What must you do if you are involved in a minor accident?*

A If possible, move the car off the road. Take the name, address and insurance details of the other driver and give him yours. Note the number plate of the other vehicle.

Q *If you break down or have an accident and are carrying a red warning triangle, how far behind the car should it be placed?*

A At least 50 metres on ordinary roads and 150 metres on the hard shoulder of a motorway.

Q *What steps would you take if you are the first to arrive at the scene of an accident?*

A 1 Warn other traffic by use of a red triangle or hazard lights.
2 Make sure all engines are switched off and there is no danger of fire.
3 Arrange for the police and ambulance to be called.
4 Give first aid and get uninjured people away from the vehicles.
5 Wait for the emergency services to arrive.

Q *What should you do if you break down on a level crossing?*

A Get the passengers out and use the telephone to tell the signalman. Only if the signalman tells you there is time do you push the car off the crossing.

Q *When driving at night, if a vehicle approaches you with its headlights on full beam, what action should you take?*

A Slow down and avert your eyes. Stop if necessary.

Q *When driving in snow, how could you tell that you have arrived at a STOP junction?*

A A STOP sign has a distinctive octagonal shape.

Q *What is the purpose of a white line along the left-hand edge of a road?*

A The line is painted in unlit areas to warn of grass verges or ditches, so you should not cross the line.

Q *What is the speed limit on an unrestricted road?*

A 60 m.p.h.

QUESTIONS ON MOTORWAY DRIVING

Q *What is the hard shoulder for?*

A Stopping in an emergency only.

Q *What is the right-hand lane for?*

A Overtaking only.

Q *Is there a fast lane?*

A No. This is a misnomer.

Q *What is a 'crawler lane'?*

A An extra lane on long hills to be used by slower vehicles.

Q *Where may you park?*
A Only in service areas.

Q *What if you break down?*
A Pull onto the hard shoulder. Put on your hazard warning lights, ensure your passengers are in no danger and go to the nearest telephone.

Q *How far apart are telephones?*
A One mile.

Q *How can you tell where the nearest telephone is?*
A There are marker posts every 100 metres with a picture of a telephone and an arrow pointing the way to the nearest.

Q *What should you do if something falls off your vehicle?*
A Go to the nearest telephone and inform the police. Do not try to retrieve it yourself.

Q *What is the speed limit?*
A Unless otherwise stated, 70 m.p.h.

Q *There are different coloured studs marking the lanes on motorways. Where are they?*
A Red studs marking the left-hand edge.
Amber studs marking the right-hand edge.
Green studs marking the acceleration and deceleration lanes.
White studs separating the lanes.

Q *What is their purpose?*
A To aid you when driving at night.

Q *What are the acceleration and deceleration lanes?*

A Extra lanes at the side which allow you to build up your speed when joining a motorway, and allow you to slow down when leaving.

Q *If you see red lights flashing over your lane, what must you do?*

A Proceed no further in that lane.

Q *What must you* not *do on a motorway?*

A Exceed 70 m.p.h.
Reverse.
Drive down the wrong side.
Cross the central reservation.
Stop on the carriageways.
Walk on the carriageways.
Stop on the hard shoulder except in an emergency.

Q *What should you take particular note of once you have left a motorway?*

A Your speed, as you may be driving faster than you think.

Q *What do the signs in Fig. 27 mean?*

A **(a)** Change lane.
(b) Leave motorway at next exit.
(c) Lane closed ahead.
(d) End of restriction.

(a)

(b)

(c)

(d)

Fig. 27

109

TRAFFIC SIGNS

Q *There are three distinct shapes of signs.
What are they and what do they mean?*

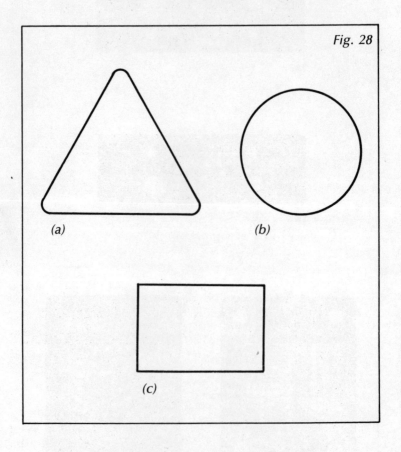

Fig. 28

(a)

(b)

(c)

A **(a)** Warning signs.
   (b) Signs giving orders.
   (c) Information signs.

Q *What do the signs in Fig. 29 mean?*

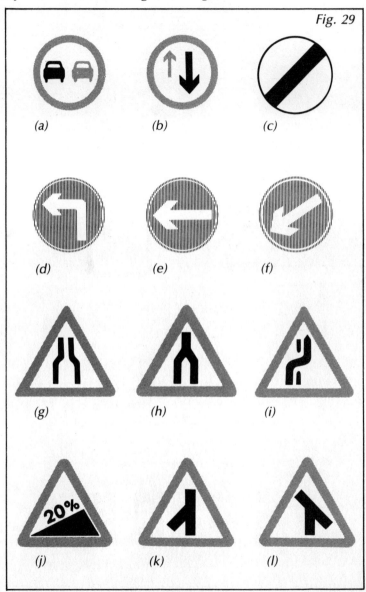

Fig. 29

(a)

(b)

(c)

(d)

(e)

(f)

(g)

(h)

(i)

(j)

(k)

(l)

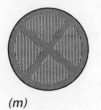
(m)

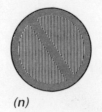
(n)

(o)

(p) Yellow border, green background

(q)

(r)

(s)

(t) Green backgrounds

A   **(a)**   No overtaking.

      (b)   Give priority to vehicles from opposite direction.

      (c)   National speed limit applies.

      (d)   Turn left ahead.

      (e)   Turn left.

      (f)   Keep left.

      (g)   Road narrows on both sides.

      (h)   Dual carriageway ends.

      (i)   Change to opposite carriageway.

      (j)   Steep hill upwards.

      (k)   Traffic merges from left with equal priority.

      (l)   Traffic merges from right with equal priority.

      (m)   No stopping (clearway).

      (n)   Parking restrictions in force.

      (o)   Priority over vehicles from opposite direction.

      (p)   Ring road on a primary route.

      (q)   Ring road on a non-primary route.

      (r)   Level crossing without barrier.

      (s)   Count-down markers at exit from a motorway.

      (t)   Count-down markers at end of a primary road.

Q *What do the road markings in Fig. 30 mean?*

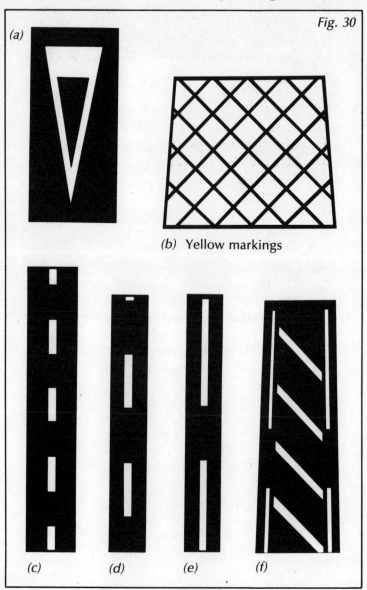

Fig. 30

(a)

(b) Yellow markings

(c) (d) (e) (f)

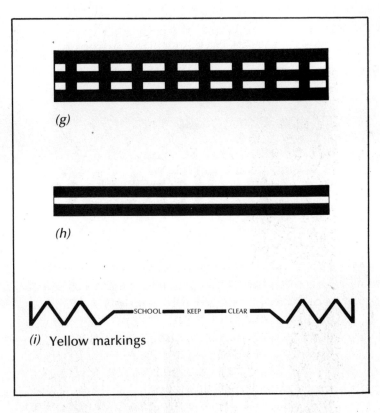

(g)

(h)

(i) Yellow markings

A (a) Warning of 'Give Way' just ahead.
   (b) Box junction.
   (c) Lane line.
   (d) Centre line.
   (e) Hazard warning line.
   (f) Chevrons — to separate streams of traffic.
   (g) Give way to traffic on major roads.
   (h) Stop line at STOP sign.
   (i) Keep entrance clear even when picking up or setting down children.

7
THE RESULT

Q *What happens when I pass?*
A The examiner will give you a pass certificate which you must send to the D.V.L.C. at Swansea together with your provisional licence and another application form. No fee is payable for this.

Q *Can I drive straight away?*
A Yes, take a note of your 'driver number' and keep it with you while your licence is away.

Q *Can I drive an automatic if I pass in a manual car?*
A Yes.

Q *Should I take more lessons?*
A All driving experience gained with a qualified instructor will stand you in good stead. It helps to drive on a motorway for the first time with an instructor and he can

show you how to reverse properly into a parking place.

Q *Should I take an advanced test?*
A Yes. If everybody took an advanced test, driving standards would undoubtedly improve. It is in your own best interest to take a pride in your driving.

Q *What should I do if I fail?*
A Apply immediately for another test. You must wait at least one calendar month before taking it again. Do not be despondent, but think carefully about where you went wrong and work at it so that you are ready for the next test.

Q *Will the examiner discuss the points on which I failed?*
A No. They are not permitted to discuss the test with you.

Q *Can I appeal against the examiner's decision?*
A The only grounds for appeal is if the test was not conducted properly. You cannot appeal against the result.

8
CONCLUSION

In this book, we have covered everything you need to know to pass a driving test, but do remember there is more to driving than simply passing the test.

There are numerous situations you will not have encountered before taking the test, and these will need to be dealt with competently and safely. Driving is a skill that you never stop learning.

Being able to drive gives you a new found freedom but also great responsibility. Whenever you get into the driving seat of a car you must realise your responsibility to yourself, your passengers and all other road users. In the wrong hands, a car can be a very dangerous weapon. Always take a pride in your driving.

Good luck.

9
NOTES
FOR AFTER
THE TEST

While learning to drive, you have probably used someone else's car — a driving school car or possibly your parents' or a friend's car. Now that you have passed, it is time to get one of your own and become truly independent. The following questions will, hopefully, set you off on the right foot.

Q   *How much should I pay for a car?*
A   Cars are expensive. A car is the second largest purchase you are likely to make in your life. Do not rush to buy the first one you see; there are very few bargains around, and you tend to get what you pay for. Work out a realistic budget before you look, and remember all the other incidentals.

Q *What are these 'other incidentals'?*

A A car must be taxed and insured. Car tax is currently £100 a year (1987) and as a new driver you may find the cost of insurance quite high. Also you must keep the car in a roadworthy condition and, unless you buy a new car, it is likely that some work will need to be done.

Q *Should I learn about car maintenance?*

A The more you know about your car the more time and money you will save yourself in the future.

Q *Should I have my car serviced by a garage?*

A Unless you feel confident in your mechanical ability, it would be better to seek the services of an expert. Having a car serviced regularly does prolong its life and probably pays for itself in the long run. If the car you buy is over three years old you must get an M.O.T. certificate once a year.

Q *How should I prepare my car for winter?*

A Check there is enough anti-freeze in the cooling system, that the tyres are not too worn, the windscreen wiper blades are functioning effectively and the lights and brakes are in full working order.

Q *What extra precautions should I take in snow?*

A If possible, keep the car in a garage when you are not using it. If you are advised by the police only to drive if your journey is vital, then only use your car if you must. If you cannot avoid driving, allow a lot longer for the journey, keep a good distance from the vehicle in front and use the brakes very gently.

Q *What about driving at night?*

A Driving at night is very different from daytime. You may not be able to see familiar landmarks and will have to follow the road signs more closely. There is, obviously, less traffic on the roads and if you are undertaking a long journey, it can be easier to do so during the night. However, you will feel sleepy so take plenty of breaks and get out of the car to stretch your legs. Pedestrians are very difficult to see at night, so keep an extra-special lookout.

Q *What if it is raining at night?*

A You will experience a lot of glare from other lights in the rain. Do not let your eyes get drawn to the lights, concentrate on the road in front of you and keep your speed down.

Q   *What is different about driving on a
motorway?*

A   The speed you will be travelling at will be a
lot higher than you have been used to up
till now. Always drive within your own
capabilities and allow yourself enough time
to get used to the speed of the other traffic
before you drive too fast yourself. Although
there is a speed limit of 70 m.p.h. on
motorways, a lot of cars are capable of 120
m.p.h. and more, and the fact is there will
be a lot of people driving faster than 70
m.p.h. What is needed is frequent checks in
the mirror and when overtaking allow
yourself plenty of time to move out and
back in.

The other point about motorway driving is
that it is very boring and your mind will
tend to wander or you may feel sleepy.
There are service stations at regular
intervals, so do not push yourself — pull in
and take a break. When leaving a motorway,
be careful to adjust your speed.

Q   *How do I park in reverse?*
A   See Fig. 31.

1   Pull up parallel to and approximately
    one metre away from the car you have
    to reverse behind. Leave the indicator
    on.
2   Reverse until your back wheels are
    opposite the rear of that car and then
    steer gently left.

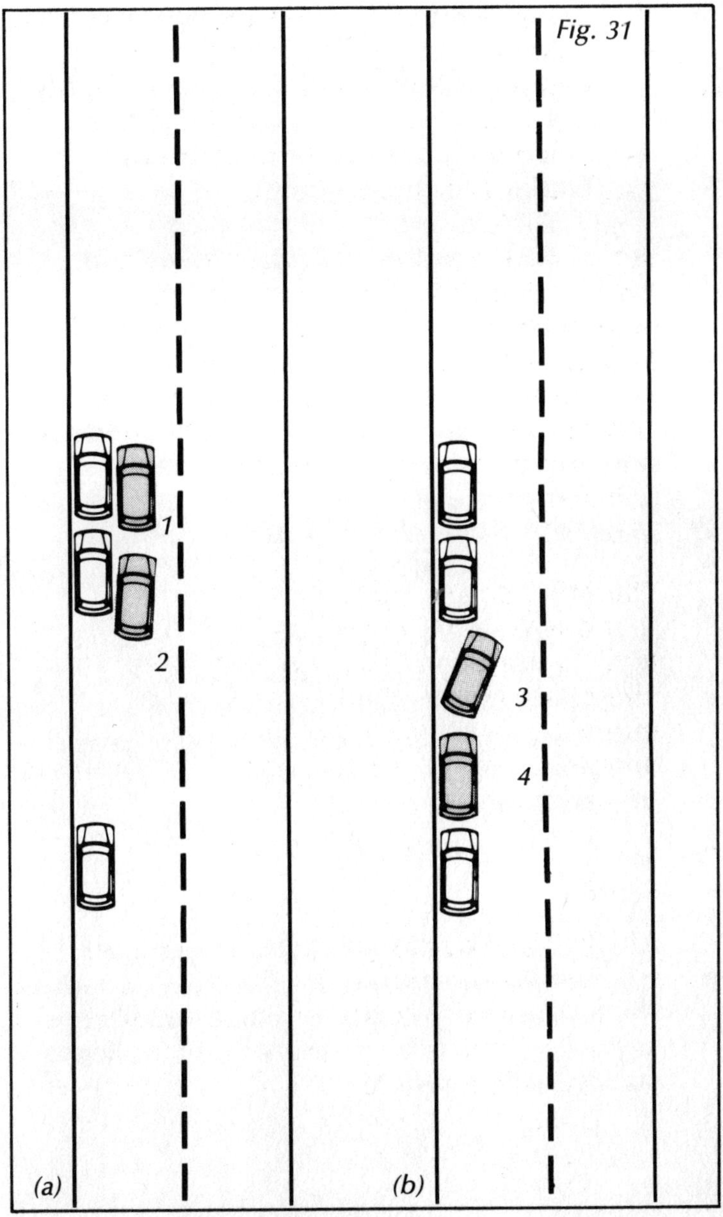

Fig. 31

(a)   (b)

123

3 When the front wheels of your car are opposite the rear of the other car, check for traffic and then steer smartly right.

4 Select first gear and move the car forward to finish neatly.

If you do the whole exercise slowly and calmly, you should find you end up satisfactorily. If you have cars waiting for you, do not let them hinder you — just concentrate on what you are doing. Practise this manoeuvre whenever you get a chance and you will soon become proficient.

Q *What essentials should I carry in the car?*
A 1 Driving licence.
2 Insurance details.
3 Spare petrol can (empty).
4 Cloth for the windows.
5 Spare bulbs for the back lights.
In addition, during the winter, also have:
1 A shovel.
2 De-icer.
3 A windscreen scraper.
4 An old coat or blanket.

Q *Must I always carry my licence with me?*
A No, but it is advisable. If you are stopped by the police and you do not have your licence with you it must be produced at a police station within five days.

Q *What should I do if I am stopped by the police?*

A The police will only stop you if they think you are committing an offence. Always be courteous; most traffic violations are minor offences and if you are polite you may only be given a verbal warning.

Q *What are the rules concerning drink/driving?*

A You must not drive with a blood alcohol level higher than 80 mg/100 ml. Different people react in different ways to drink and it is better not to drink at all if you are driving. Drink/driving is a very serious offence and the very least you will get away with is a large fine and the loss of your licence.

Notes

Notes

Notes